Opening the World of Learning™

A COMPREHENSIVE EARLY LITERACY PROGRAM

Evaluating Language and Literacy in Four-Year-Olds:
A Practical Guide for Teachers

Barbara DeBaryshe, Ph.D.

Dana Gorecki, M.Ed

Judy Schickedanz, Ph.D.

David Dickinson, Ed.D.

in collaboration with
Charlotte-Mecklenburg Schools

PEARSON EARLY LEARNING
Pearson Learning Group

Art and Design: Stephen Barth, Robert Dobaczewski, Sherri Hieber-Day, David Mager, Judy Mahoney, Elbaliz Mendez, Jim O'Shea, Dan Trush, Jennifer Visco, Heather Wendt Kemp

Editorial: Diane Arnell, Danielle Camaleri, Teri Crawford Jones, Jaime Dritt, Deborah Eaton, Mary Lou Mackin, Susan Poskanzer

Inventory: Levon Carter, Jeff Hoitsma

Marketing: Diane Bradley, Laura Egan

Production/Manufacturing: Karen Edmonds, Nathan Kinney, Jennifer McCormack

Publishing Operations: Carolyn Coyle, Richetta Lobban

ISBN 1-57212-758-9

Printed in the United States of America

    6 7 8 9 10   08

Opening the World of Learning™ is a trademark of Pearson Education, Inc.

Pearson
Early
Learning

Pearson Learning Group

1-800-321-3106
www.pearsonlearning.com
www.pearsonearlylearning.com

CONTENTS

Rubrics Assessment and Instructional Decision Making

Effective early childhood teachers are aware of the developmental levels of all children in their classrooms and make adjustments in their instructional program in response to children's needs. The most effective instruction occurs when teachers make adjustments based on sound knowledge of children's developmental levels. As they seek to engage and teach children, teachers will find the flexibility they need to make adjustments with the books and activities provided by *Opening the World of Learning: A Comprehensive Early Literacy Program™ (OWL)*.

To support teachers' efforts to individualize instruction, *Evaluating Language and Literacy in Four-Year-Olds: A Practical Guide for Teachers* provides an ongoing observational assessment tool of children's language and literacy skills and behaviors. It is intended to ascertain an individual child's status at a point in time as well as his or her progress over time.

The guide consists of rubrics that are grouped into four domains: *Oral Language, Book Interest and Understanding, Phonological Awareness,* and *Print Understanding and Use.* Within each domain there are two to five areas of development. For each of these areas of development there is a rubric that describes sets of behaviors that reflect different levels of accomplishment (*beginning, consolidating, proficient*). The rubrics can be found on pages 6–20 in this guide.

The rubrics guide teachers to think in a comprehensive way about the abilities that children are developing that support early literacy. This set of rubrics is designed to help teachers look at the variety of things children do in the course of the classroom day and interpret the clues children provide about their development in different areas of literacy.

The insights gained from the rubrics serve as good starting points for teachers to think about what they might do to engage a child more fully with the curriculum. The activity plans that are a part of the curriculum in *Opening the World of Learning* make useful suggestions for a variety of children, including English Language Learners, those who need extra support, and those who are ready for additional challenges. By using these suggestions along with their own professional judgment, teachers can make adjustments to meet children's instructional needs.

For example, based on the rubrics, a teacher may note that a child rarely engages in pretend play that involves literacy tools. As a result, the teacher might model uses of literacy tools by joining the child in the pretend restaurant and pretending to be a customer who wants to order. The teacher could ask for a menu (which would be available), pretend to read it, and then coach the child in taking an order. For example, the teacher might say, *How can you remember everything? Wouldn't it be good to write my order down?* Later in the week, the teacher could briefly observe the child to see if the child was shifting his or her play to include greater use of literacy tools. If not, the teacher could model play with literacy tools again in the pretend restaurant or during another activity.

Domains	Areas of Development	Behavioral Indicators
Oral Language	Vocabulary	the size and nature of vocabulary and interest in learning new words
	Conversation	the ability to engage in effective back-and-forth exchanges of experiences, ideas, and opinions
	Using Language to Resolve Conflicts	the ability to de-escalate conflicts and resolve conflicts by effective use of language
	Using Language to Tell Personal Narratives and Engage in Pretend Play	skills in telling stories about personal experiences; the ability to engage in sustained pretending in dramatic play that includes dialogue
	Using Language to Learn Information and How to Do Things	the facility in using language to learn by listening and asking questions, and the ability to engage in high-level thinking such as forming hypotheses
Book Interest and Understanding	Interest in Books	interest in and the ability to attend to different kinds of books
	Understanding of and Responses to Books	the ability to understand different kinds of books and to respond to them in appropriate ways
Phonological Awareness	Syllable Awareness	the ability to identify syllable boundaries and divide words into syllables
	Beginning Sounds	the ability to identify the first phoneme in words and to use that awareness to sort words and relate initial sounds to letters
	Rhyme Awareness	the ability to identify and produce rhymes
	Phonemic Awareness	the ability to attend to phonemes in different parts of a word, to divide spoken words into phonemes, and for some sounds to relate the sound to the letter or letters that represent it
Print Understanding and Use	Meaning and Uses of Print	the ability to understand how print conveys meaning and awareness of the varied uses of print
	Early Writing	the ability to form letters and to use print in conventional ways to represent sounds and communicate meaning
	Early Reading	understanding of what reading is and emerging ability to attend to and interpret print in the environment and in books
	Alphabet Letter Knowledge	knowledge of the shapes and names of letters and emerging understanding of the sounds that some letters represent

Oral Language

Skill	Rubric Level		
	Beginning	**Consolidating**	**Proficient**
Vocabulary The number, variety, and complexity of words the child understands and uses	Vocabulary is smaller and less varied than that of most children of the same age.	Vocabulary size and richness is typical for most children of the same age.	Vocabulary is markedly larger and more varied than that of most children of the same age. Child displays interest in and enthusiasm for learning new words.

	Beginning	Consolidating	Proficient
	• Child often is unaware of the meanings of words used as a part of classroom conversations. • Words used are mostly limited to objects, events, and routines that are a regular part of the child's daily experiences. • Child uses familiar phrases repeatedly (e.g., "Help me," or "I want that") with little variation in word choice. • Child often must rely heavily on gestures or facial expressions to express meaning. • Child may get frustrated, withdrawn, or give up easily because of a lack of words to communicate meaning.	• Child understands a variety of words used in books that refer to animals (e.g., farm animals, animals often seen in zoos), objects (e.g., different vehicles, tools, buildings) and places (e.g., types of stores, zoo, school, doctor's office) familiar to many children of his or her age. • Child understands some less common verbs and descriptive words, but often is not familiar with words not heard in everyday speech. • Child has the vocabulary to talk about classroom objects, routines, and events freely. • Child uses words to describe different actions, but words tend to be the most common, basic words (e.g., *fell down*, not *crashed* or *tumbled*; *hit*, not *smashed* or *whacked*). • Child uses descriptive words, but words tend to be basic, common adjectives and adverbs (e.g., *bad*, not *horrible*; *pretty*, not *magnificent*). • Child sometimes spontaneously uses new key vocabulary words appropriately, but most often in sentences similar to those he or she has heard in books.	• Child understands many words that are not heard in common speech. For example, the child often already understands many words identified as key vocabulary in books. • Child uses a wide variety of words, including rare or unusual words and names for animals and objects (e.g., *Triceratops, fire extinguisher*). Varied nouns may reflect areas of special interest to the child (e.g., *dinosaurs, dogs*). • Child uses verbs (e.g., *construct, escape, consider*), adjectives (e.g., *slick, enticing, delectable*), and adverbs (e.g., *cleverly, rapidly*) that are not common in everyday conversations. • Child often uses key vocabulary words spontaneously, sometimes in sentences and situations quite different from those experienced in the book. • Child displays interest in new words and spontaneously comments on novel words heard in books or conversations.

Oral Language

Skill	Rubric Level		
	Beginning	**Consolidating**	**Proficient**
Conversation The ability to engage with other people in back-and-forth discussion Conversational partners take turns acting as speaker and listener, exchanging information, questions and/or comments about the same topic.	Child engages in conversations reluctantly.	Child initiates conversations and engages in back-and-forth discussions.	Child actively engages in lengthy, varied, and complex conversations.

Beginning

- Child is generally unwilling to start conversations with others and often starts nonverbally (e.g., Rather than asking for help, child places an untied shoe in an adult's lap.).
- If child tries to start a conversation and is not understood or fails to get the attention of the listener, he or she gives up quickly.
- Conversations with other children are short, with only two to three back-and-forth exchanges.
- Conversations with adults are largely directed by adult prompting. Child is better at answering questions than he or she is at asking questions to extend the conversation.

Consolidating

- Child starts conversations with familiar peers or adults, but may not be comfortable with both.
- Child will rephrase what he or she says using different words if others do not understand.
- Conversations with adults vary in length, but tend to be brief with other children except when engaged in dramatic play.
- Child asks some questions and makes comments that help keep the discussion flowing (e.g., "I love horses. What's your favorite animal?").

Proficient

- Child frequently and confidently starts conversations with peers and adults about a variety of topics.
- Child participates in a conversation with peers and adults for multiple exchanges and stays on topic.
- Child can share ideas and experiences as an equal conversational partner in a conversation with peers or adults.
- Child reveals understanding of the points of view of other speakers (e.g., "William said, . . . but I . . ."; "I hadn't thought of that!").
- Child asks questions and makes comments that keep the discussion going.

Oral Language

Skill	Rubric Level		
	Beginning	**Consolidating**	**Proficient**
Using Language to Resolve Conflicts The ability to state his or her point of view and use language to resolve conflicts	Child often resorts to nonverbal means to resolve conflicts.	Child uses language to describe own position in conflict situations and begins to use language to solve problems.	Child uses language to negotiate and resolve conflicts.
	• Child uses nonverbal communication (pushes others, takes toys back) or simple verbal commands ("No." Or, "Don't.") to protest or assert position. • Child may use short commands to assert position (e.g., "No, that's mine!" Or, "Stop doing that."). • Child has limited ability to label his or her emotions. • Child is a passive bystander to other children's conflicts.	• Child labels own emotions using basic labels (e.g., "I'm mad," "I'm angry," or "I don't like you."). • Child states what or why he or she is protesting (e.g., "Stop that, I'm playing with the blocks."). • Child explains own emotional state or position (e.g., "I'm really mad that you drew on my paper."). • When describing conflicts to others, child focuses on the negative actions of the other child. • When witnessing a peer conflict, child will ask a teacher to intervene (e.g., "Teacher! Brianna and Jerry are fighting.").	• Child will use reasoning, extended arguments, and/or negotiation to resolve conflicts (e.g., "I'm playing with the blocks now. You can have them later." Or, "I'm really tired now, Miss. I just can't get up and put that away now."). • Child describes and explains own emotional states, going beyond basic emotional terms (e.g., "You're sitting too close. You bother me. Move over." Or, "Be quiet! You're hurting my ears."). • Child will intervene verbally in peer conflicts to ask what is going on or to defend a peer (e.g., "What's wrong?" "That's her toy." or "Stop fighting!"). Intervention is limited to one or two questions or commands.

Oral Language

Skill	Rubric Level		
	Beginning	**Consolidating**	**Proficient**
Using Language to Tell Personal Narratives and Engage in Pretend Play The ability to give a coherent and accurate recounting of past events or personal stories and to create and enact roles as part of dramatic play	Child tells rudimentary narratives and makes limited use of language as part of pretend play.	Child tells partial narratives and uses language as part of dramatic play.	Child tells reasonably complete narratives and uses language to create novel dramatic-play scenarios.

• Child's stories include two past events (e.g., "I had a party and we ate ice cream."). • The events within a story may not clearly be related or in the correct order (e.g., "The puppy was jumping and I played with a puzzle."). • Child shares personal narratives if an adult gives step-by-step prompts (e.g., "What did you do in school today?" "Played." "What did you play with?" "Puzzles." "What kind of puzzles?" "The monkey puzzle and the boat one."). • When pretending, the child uses sound effects and isolated words or draws on language from very familiar routines (e.g., "Feed the baby." Or, "I'm sleepy.").	• Child's stories include more than two past events (e.g., "I went to Grandma's house. Papa fixed the car. We had lots of fun."). • Child often leaves out details needed to understand the story or tells events out of sequence (e.g., "She was crying. She tried to make her feel better. Mommy, Judy, Beth and me was all there."). • Child often requires several prompts to complete a narrative or provide the listener with crucial detail (e.g., "What did you do in school today?" "We played with blocks." "Tell me more." "I played with Tommy in the block corner. We made a tower."). • Child negotiates roles with other children and engages in pretend play using dialogue. Conversations include familiar story lines (e.g., After *Noisy Nora* is read several times, children reenact the book.).	• Child tells multiple-event stories in which the events are generally given in the correct order and enough detail is given for the listener to understand what happened (e.g., "We went to the park. I pushed my sister on the swings. There was lots of kids there. A dog chased me. And we went to get pizza."). • Child shares narratives with few prompts from adults (e.g., "What did you do in school today?" "We talked about insects. They have six legs and walk funny. And I drew a picture of a grasshopper in my journal." "What else did you do?" "We sang songs. Ate snacks. Had lunch. Naptime. That's all."). • Child creates and enacts roles and extended scenarios that are novel (e.g., pretends to be trying to find a missing dinosaur and has a series of adventures). Child can sustain dramatic play for extended periods of time (15 minutes or more).

Oral Language

Skill	Rubric Level		
	Beginning	**Consolidating**	**Proficient**
Using Language to Learn Information and How to Do Things The ability to learn new information and to learn new ways of doing things from language	Child's use and understanding of language is grounded in the immediate present or relies on well-learned routines.	Child's use and understanding of language draws on a balance of language alone and language plus supports; conversation may not be tied to the present.	Child is able to use language to learn and to gain information with limited reliance on support of objects, gestures, and familiar routines.
	• Topics of conversation are almost always linked to concrete objects, ongoing activities, or statements about needs or desires. Child does not talk about the meanings of words or ideas. • Child cannot understand new activities or routines without gestures or visual cues, and needs such supports to learn new ideas. • Child asks for basic information (e.g., "What color is that?" "What are we doing today?" or "Where are you going?"). Child may ask the meaning of words naming concrete objects.	• Topics of conversation include talk about past and future activities and occasionally child's ideas and beliefs (e.g., "I think the leaves fall down because it's windy."). Child may talk about language. For example, child may note different names for the same thing in two languages, and may comment on word meanings or the sounds of words. • Child asks questions to gain more complex information (e.g., Child starts to ask "why" and "how" questions.). When he or she hears an unfamiliar word, the child will often ask what it means. • Child can follow directions about familiar routines that have multiple steps (e.g., "Go use the bathroom, wash your hands, and then line up to go outside."). • Child needs visual prompts to know how to do new activities or procedures (e.g., Child can follow directions for a new craft activity if the teacher both explains and demonstrates the steps.). • Child can learn new concepts when a definition or explanation is given in terms of familiar experiences (e.g., The teacher explains what *excitement* is by referring to specific times when child displayed that emotion.).	• Child often spontaneously uses language to state hypotheses, to speculate about the reasons why things happen (e.g., "I think the roots suck up the water."), or to talk about language or new information he or she has learned. • Child will ask a series of questions and may realize when more information or clarification is needed (e.g., Child asks for repetition or says, "I don't understand."). • Child learns new concepts through words alone and freely participates in discussion of things that are unfamiliar, are not physically present, or are about ideas or the meanings of words. • Child can carry out simple new activities or procedures based on verbal directions alone (e.g., how to water a plant correctly without needing the teacher to model as he or she explains the procedure).

Book Interest and Understanding

Skill	Rubric Level		
	Beginning	**Consolidating**	**Proficient**
Interest in Books The degree to which the child enjoys a variety of age-appropriate books and seeks opportunities to look at books or be read to	Child shows low to moderate interest, with engagement only during read-aloud times.	Child shows moderate to high interest during read-aloud times and occasional independent engagement with books.	Child shows consistently high interest during read-aloud times and frequent independent engagement with books.
	• Child sustains attention for an entire book only when it is a familiar predictable book. • Child asks to be read to or looks at books independently but does so mostly during scheduled book-reading or library-use times (e.g., The child participates in classroom story time but does not usually select books during free play.). • Child shows interest in a small selection of favorite books, but sometimes fidgets or does not appear to enjoy being read to. Child shows interest most often with familiar predictable books.	• Child sustains attention during short- to medium-length storybooks or to multiple shorter books. • Child engages with books on a daily basis in addition to regularly scheduled story times (e.g., Child looks at books available in play areas, visits the class library, asks to be read to and/or shares books with friends.). • Child enjoys an increasing number and variety of books. • Child enjoys listening to both familiar and unfamiliar books.	• Child sustains attention for virtually all books. He or she sustains attention for several stories in one sitting. • Child uses multiple opportunities to use books throughout the day, and often engages peers or a teacher in book use. • The library area is among child's preferred play areas. Child often engages peers in looking at books, and also engages deeply with books when alone. • Child enjoys a wide number and variety of books. • Child often initiates conversations about books at times other than during book reading.

Book Interest and Understanding

Skill	Rubric Level		
	Beginning	**Consolidating**	**Proficient**
Understanding of and Responses to Books The ability to follow and understand as a book is read aloud, and to participate in book-related conversations that support the development of vocabulary and story comprehension	Child attends to conversations of others about a book, or participates minimally in basic conversations about familiar books.	Child readily participates in book-related conversations and sometimes applies knowledge gained from a book to new situations.	Child participates in elaborate and extended book-related conversations and often applies knowledge gained from books to new situations.

• Child responds to basic questions and prompts during story-reading, by pointing, answering "yes" or "no," or naming characters and simple objects in the pictures. • Child goes beyond comments about illustrations that show little attention to the text the teacher reads by asking "who" and "what" questions about characters, objects, and events. Child also makes short comments about the pictures (e.g., "He's scary!" or "I like that one!").	• Child answers a wider variety of questions that requires him or her to name or describe characters, objects, and events shown in the pictures (e.g., "What is she doing?" "How many bears are in the woods?" or "What colors do you see?"). • Child may answer more complex questions about both the pictures and the plot (e.g., "Why does he look so angry?" or "What will he do now?"). • Child asks questions and makes comments about characters and the plot, and sometimes mentions pictures. • Child may ask for explanations and may draw links between the book and his or her experiences (e.g., "Why is Peter taking his baby picture?" or "I saw a tiger like that at the circus.").	• Child consistently answers a wide range of complex questions about both characters and plot. • Child's answers are often lengthy and use background knowledge and experiences (e.g., "No, you couldn't really keep a baby whale in your bathtub. When it grows up, it's too big. You need an ocean. This book is just pretend."). • Child's answers also frequently refer to the story text (e.g., ". . . because it said the pictures fell off the walls"). • Child poses questions frequently, which are often sophisticated and insightful, and enjoys extended discussions about books. • Child often talks about things that can be inferred from the text, but are not directly evident in the pictures or the text (e.g., "Maybe Peter thought he might get a new chair if he gave his baby chair to his sister." or "Maybe Baby Louise wanted Daniel to take her outside with him to play."). • Child notes unfamiliar ideas, concepts or facts, and asks many questions about and/or comments on this unfamiliar content.

Phonological Awareness

Skill	Rubric Level		
	Beginning	**Consolidating**	**Proficient**
Syllable Awareness The ability to divide words into syllables or blend syllables to form a whole word	Child divides or blends two-syllable words with teacher support.	Child divides or blends familiar words with two to three syllables consistently. Recognizes syllables within longer, unfamiliar words with assistance.	Child divides and blends syllables, including lengthy words that are novel, independently.

Syllables are the major parts or beats inside words; each syllable is marked by a slight drop in the speaker's jaw.

One-syllable words:

　bed

　stop

Two-syllable words:

　mommy

　turtle

Three-syllable words:

　December

　photograph

- Child claps along with the teacher as she models one- and two-syllable words or compound words (e.g., *baby*: *ba* [clap], *by* [clap]).

- Child can blend two syllables to make a familiar word when supported by a picture or object (e.g., Child sees two to three pictures, and correctly points to the item when asked, "Where is the kit-ten?").

- When another person says a familiar two- or three-syllable word, the child accurately claps out the syllables (e.g., "fur-ni-ture," "e-nor-mous").

- Without assistance, child sorts pictures of familiar objects (e.g., cat, tree, house, table, banana, umbrella, telephone) into groups of one-, two-, and three-syllable words.

- Child can blend familiar two-syllable words (e.g., The teacher says, "Pe-ter," "mar-ble.").

- Child can independently clap out syllables in words of three or more syllables.

- Child comments that some words have more syllables than others (e.g., "*Pumpkin* is longer than *cat*.").

- Child is consistently accurate in blending familiar words of two to four syllables.

Phonological Awareness

Skill	Rubric Level		
	Beginning	**Consolidating**	**Proficient**
Beginning Sound Awareness The ability to segment the first sound in a word (Note: The initial sound may be represented by one or two letters.)	Child begins to attend to initial sounds.	Child recognizes and isolates beginning sounds.	Child generates some words that start with the same sound, including those in words starting with a single consonant phoneme or a consonant blend.
For example: bed, /b/ hamster, /h/ ship, /sh/ thumb, /th/ string, /s/ acorn, /ā/	• Child enjoys listening to alphabet books, poems, and rhymes with alliteration (repeated initial sounds: *Wee Willie Winkie; Diddle, Diddle, Dumpling; Peas Porridge Hot, Peas Porridge Cold*). • Child sings familiar songs and retells predictable books that have text that repeats the same sound across a series of words or in the same line or verse of a poem, book, or song. • Child notices that two words begin with the same sound. This may occur first for their names, but is seen for other words also. • Child repeats stretching out of phonemes heard in words in stories, songs, or poems (e.g., mimics *baarrroooom* from *One Dark Night*, or *Shhhhhhhh* from *Peter's Chair*). • When writing, child often repeats an initial sound, and in words in which a teacher isolates the initial sound after child has asked how to spell (e.g., the teacher says, "ssstore" to help child hear /s/).	• Child can think of another word or two that starts with the same sound as a word the teacher says. • Child can find objects in the classroom, or point out pictures on a poster or in a book that have names that start with a target sound (e.g., all the things that start /m/). • Child can begin to isolate initial sounds alone (e.g., the child asks the teacher how to spell *love*. The teacher asks, "What sound do you hear first in *love*?" Child says the word slowly, identifies the /l/ sound and says, "L!").	• For nearly all words, child can isolate initial sounds and easily gives examples of word pairs or word lists that start with these sounds. • When supported, the child can often write letters that reflect isolation of initial sounds. • On occasion, child writes letters that reflect independent isolation of initial sounds without assistance or encouragement. • Given six to eight pictures of familiar objects, child can match pairs with names that begin with the same sound.

Phonological Awareness

Skill	Rubric Level		
	Beginning	**Consolidating**	**Proficient**
Rhyme Awareness The ability to hear, recognize, and generate words that rhyme	Child begins to notice and copy rhyming words, but does not yet identify or produce rhymes.	Child recognizes and identifies rhyming words heard in poems, books, and songs even when an adult has not yet pointed them out.	Child easily and spontaneously produces rhymes, including multi-syllabic words.

Rhyming words have the same set of sounds from the vowel to the end of the last syllable.

For example:

c-at, f-at, h-at

do, too, you, Sue

str-ing, s-ing, r-ing

Beginning

- Child repeats pairs of rhyming words spoken by another person.
- Child attends to books, poems, songs, etc., that include rhyme, in a way that indicates awareness of the special quality of the language (e.g., Upon hearing a rhyme, child smiles or is more attentive than usual.).
- Child sings rhyming songs, recites rhyming chants, and fingerplays.
- Child fills in rhyming words in a familiar poem or book when teacher pauses.
- Child can guess what word the teacher is saying when the word is said slowly and divided into the onset (all sounds before the first vowel) and rime (the first vowel and all subsequent sounds) (e.g., b- [pause] *ike*, c- [pause] *ar*, st- pause *op*, w- [pause] *ater*.)

Consolidating

- Child produces rhymes when he or she hears two words that rhyme, or when rhyming words are called to child's attention (e.g., After reading a line in a predictable book, the teacher notes that *sun* and *run* rhyme and child comments that *fun* rhymes also.).
- Child typically offers only one or two additional rhyming words.
- Child consistently recognizes when words rhyme, even if words are unfamiliar.
- Child can match six to eight pictures into pairs of rhyming words. For example, child can find pairs when given six or eight pictures of pairs of objects that rhyme (e.g., *egg, leg; hen, pen; hog, log; cat, rat*).
- If told a list of three words, child can indicate the two that rhyme or the one that does not. Child asks questions or seeks feedback on whether words rhyme.

Proficient

- When asked, child easily produces lists of rhyming words, including real and nonsense words (e.g., *do, goo, foo, you, zoo; namby, pamby, camby, lamby*).
- Child spontaneously generates rhyming words without prompting or having heard rhyming text or rhyming pairs.
- Child is consistently correct when playing games, such as bingo or Concentration, using rhyming pairs and can sort large sets of words into groups that rhyme.

Phonological Awareness

Skill	Rubric Level		
	Beginning	**Consolidating**	**Proficient**
Phonemic Awareness The ability to hear, isolate, and manipulate the phonemes (individual sounds) that make up words	Child recognizes and identifies beginning and final sounds of single-syllable CVC words. Begins to change phonemes found at the beginning of the words. Starts to generate final sounds and blend phonemes.	Child consistently recognizes and generates final sounds. Starts to recognize and generate medial sounds. Begins to change phonemes found at the end of the words. Segments and blends words of three to four phonemes.	Child is able to detect nearly all short vowels in spoken words, and represents these when writing words. When child writes, child uses the look of the word as a check on thoroughness of phoneme segmentation. Represents correctly some phonemes that have no letter name match.

English has 43 phonemes. These phonemes are listed in most dictionaries.

Most often, a phoneme corresponds to a single letter (e.g. /m/ as in *man* or /t/ as in *tugboat*. Some phonemes, however, are represented by two letters (e.g. /sh/ as in *ship*). Some phonemes can be represented with more than one letter (e.g., /k/ as in *kite* or *cat*). Sometimes different phonemes are represented by the same letter (e.g., /a/ as in *hat*, or /ā/ as in *hate*).

Beginning

- Child can isolate initial sounds alone (e.g., Child asks the teacher how to spell *love*. The teacher asks, "What sound do you hear first in *love*?" The child says the word slowly, identifies the /l/ sound and says, "L!").

- Child can change initial consonants to make new words (e.g., If asked to change the /p/ in *pan* to /m/, he or she creates *man*.

- Child recognizes final sounds. When the teacher is with a small group and is writing a list of things to buy and comes to *paint,* she writes *PAIN* [saying sounds as she writes]. When she comes to the final sound, she says the word distinctly and pauses, and child says "/t/, that's T.").

- When prompted, child can orally blend words of three to four phonemes (e.g., /f/ /i/ /sh/, "FISH." /t/ /o͞o/ /th/, "TOOTH.").

- When writing independently, child may represent words with initial and final sounds (e.g., *t* for *boat*).

- Child notices, asks about, or comments on the sounds inside his or her own name or other familiar words.

Consolidating

- Child independently recognizes most or all final sounds in both short and longer words, and shows this knowledge in a variety of modes (e.g., comments *kite* and *bite* sound the same at the end; writes a letter for a final sound in words when there is a letter name match to the sound).

- Child writes letters that reflect independent isolation of initial sounds without assistance or encouragement.

- When prompted, child can orally segment words of three to four phonemes (e.g., tells the teacher all the sounds in the word [e.g., *spot* is /s/ /p/ /o/ /t/]).

- Child can sometimes change final consonants of words to create new words.

- When writing or using magnetic letters or letter tiles, child consistently represents first and last sounds, and usually represents one or more medial sounds (e.g., writes *kit* for *kite*, *str* for *sister*, *btl* for *bottle*).

Proficient

- Child consistently isolates the short vowels in spoken words and provides reasonable letters to represent short vowels when sounding out words on own.

- Child often asks an adult what letter to use to represent a short vowel child has isolated when sounding out a word to spell it.

- After representing sounds isolated in a word child is spelling, child asks the adult if something more is needed when the written word is missing vowels.

- Child begins to code high frequency sounds for which there is no letter-name match (e.g., uses *th*, *sh*, *ch*).

Print Understanding and Use

Skill	Rubric Level		
	Beginning	**Consolidating**	**Proficient**
Meaning and Uses of Print Understanding that print is a distinct system that is used for many purposes	Child shows initial understanding of print/picture distinction and beginning awareness of the uses of print.	Child shows understanding of print as a separate set of symbols, use of print as part of play, and recognition of varied uses of books.	Child shows understanding of many of the uses of print, skill incorporating print in multiple ways, and skill using reference books to gain information.
	• Child reveals awareness of picture/print distinction. (e.g., Child names items in a picture, with non-reading voice register and responds to print in reading voice register. Child may say, "See the picture I drawed of me?" and later say, "Jeffrey," when pointing to a scribbled signature). • Child uses literacy props with adult prompting and/or in imitation of other's play (e.g., If asked or encouraged to, child will pretend to use a telephone book or menu and will scribble a phone message). • Child may role-play people whose jobs involve print (e.g., a librarian or mail carrier), but this play does not highlight the role of print (e.g., The child may deliver mail, but does not address or read envelopes.). • Child recognizes that the same book tells a particular story or that a familiar sign or poster has a particular message. • Child protests if a highly familiar book is read incorrectly, or if the reader skips portions or makes up new content of a familiar, but non-predictable story. • Child knows that books and other print can provide information (e.g., Child who has just found an unfamiliar insect asks the teacher to "Look this up in a book.").	• Child clearly and explicitly distinguishes pictures from drawings (e.g., consistently uses the words *draw* and *write* correctly between drawing and writing). • Child usually distinguishes letters from numbers and may note differences between how different languages are written (e.g., Chinese characters versus English letters). • Child is aware of a variety of uses and genres of print (e.g., pretends to read directions in a dramatic-play cookbook, takes a message in scribble when answering a dramatic-play phone, contributes ideas to class lists). • Child spontaneously creates writing and attempts "reading" during dramatic play when appropriate props and familiar roles are provided (e.g., Child addresses and stamps envelopes in the post office center, pretends to read a road map, or "writes" a prescription using materials provided). • Child continues to request that adults read books to provide information he or she needs, and child often directs adults to specific books that have information of the kind the child requests.	• Child identifies print as print, even in unusual fonts where decorative aspects combine picture and print features. • Child knows that symbols making up writing can take many forms, and that these differ across languages (e.g., Child recognizes Hebrew, Chinese, or Arabic writing as "writing," even though marks differ dramatically from English letters.). • Child names many different forms of writing (e.g., menu, grocery list, checkbook, receipt, newspaper, magazine, greeting card, letter, recipe, map) and asks for or creates some of these for use in dramatic play. • Child frequently creates writing and responds to print in a wide variety of free-play settings. If props are not provided, child will collect materials needed or make props (e.g., Child leaves the Blocks area to get writing supplies to make street signs to place in his or her block city). • Child attempts to gather information from books and other forms of print, and asks an adult to read something specific (e.g., Child looks through a field guide and finds a picture of an insect that matches one found. Child says to the adult, "Read this part here.").

Print Understanding and Use

Skill	Rubric Level		
	Beginning	**Consolidating**	**Proficient**
Early Writing The degree to which the marks the child uses to create writing is print that can be read by others	Child makes early approximations to letters, broad distinction between print and pictures, and uses simple visual approach to making words with letters.	Child gains control of how to produce many shapes that are letter-like, and learns to write some actual letters. Child begins to link letters to sounds heard in words.	Child becomes skilled forming many letters, and gains confidence using letters to represent sounds, when attempting to spell words.
	• Child arranges markings (e.g., continuous looped or zigzag scribble, discontinuous scribble, mock letters) intended to serve as writing in horizontal or vertical sets of lines. • When creating writing that accompanies a scribbled or representative drawing, child's writing marks are separated from the marks that constitute the picture. • Child may create recognizable letter approximation for first letter in own name, and perhaps other letters. • Child may string letters together to look like words, but does not realize that letters relate to sounds of spoken words (e.g., Child writes *DLASP*, and asks, "What word is that?" or writes *SFPEZ* and *SDPO*, in list form, and says, "That's my grocery list.").	• Child's writing includes a few mock letters, many approximations to actual letters, and a few correctly formed letters. • Child writes his or her own name using many letter approximations and some correctly formed letters. Some letters may be reversed or upside down. • Child may intersperse some lowercase letters among mostly uppercase letters, especially when writing his or her name. • In play contexts, child's writing may include scribble, mock letters, approximations to actual letters, and some well-formed letters. • When an adult helps with a word the child wants to spell, child attends closely as the adult segments sounds in the word and identifies some letters based on the sounds heard. • When writing independently, child often segments words into syllables and may match letters to the first sound in the first syllable, using letter-name knowledge to select letters.	• Child writes recognizable uppercase letters and some lowercase letters. • Letters in child's name are well formed, and may include lowercase after the initial uppercase letter. Child's name may still contain reversed letters. • Even in play contexts, child often writes correctly formed letters. • Child independently isolates first and last sounds, and uses letter-name knowledge to guide selection of letters. • Child uses knowledge of how to spell some sounds to guide letter selection when writing the same sounds in other words (e.g., Charles spells *cherry* as *CHRE*; Anthony spells *apple* as *APL.*). • Child may write several common words from memory, without sounding them out (e.g., [a sibling's name], *The End, love, mom*).

Print Understanding and Use

Skill	Rubric Level		
	Beginning	**Consolidating**	**Proficient**
Early Reading Understanding of print conventions (such as book handling and tracking print), the level of emergent readings of storybooks, and attention to and strategies for reading print in the environment	Child gains book handling skills, begins to understand how print conveys meaning in books, and begins to notice and interpret environmental print.	Child understands how books are read and that print communicates particular messages. Child relies on memory of stories to "read" words using context and some letter cues.	Child understands details of how print communicates meaning. Child uses different strategies to gain meaning from print, drawing heavily on letter cues and knowledge of sight words.

Beginning

- Child relies on pictures to prompt recall of the text about a familiar storybook. The language used sounds more like conversation than book language (e.g., The child says, "The baby Louise was really, really mad. She cried so hard. And look, the pictures are falling!").

- Child realizes that people attend to print, not pictures, when reading (e.g., points to some of the print when asked what the adult reads).

- Child holds books right-side up and turns pages from front to back; may not turn one page at a time.

- Child is not aware that printed words convey meanings precisely (e.g., Child says "toothpaste" when print on tube shows a brand name).

- Child recognizes some environmental print and labels (e.g., a store name or *STOP*).

- Child comments and asks about print in a variety of contexts (e.g., nametags on cubbies, *EXIT* sign above the door, print on T-shirt).

- Child reads own name and might recognize the printed names of a few friends.

Consolidating

- When doing emergent reading of short familiar storybooks, child relies on pictures and memory. Child's language is similar to the text—much of the text is related verbatim.

- When looking at books, child starts at the front of the book and turns pages one at a time (e.g., If asked to, "Show me where I start reading," the child points to the top of the page, chart, or sign.).

- When asked to demonstrate how to track print, child runs his or her finger left to right across the print and moves globally, from the top to the bottom of the page, often skipping down several lines.

- When doing emergent reading, child often runs finger under print, sometimes pointing to salient words and may note words that the teacher pointed out when reading the book (e.g., *barrooom* in *One Dark Night*).

- Child recognizes some common printed words by sight (e.g., *Mom, Dad, No*).

- Child uses multiple cues such as pictures, object's location, and first-letter cues to guess the meaning of printed words (e.g., Child matches a card with the written word *dog* to a picture of a dog, based on child's noticing of /d/ at the beginning of the spoken word and child's knowledge of this letter name.).

Proficient

- With longer and more complex familiar storybooks, child recites the story from memory, using picture clues to prompt recall.

- With a short and simple storybook, child looks at the print and attempts to find words that he or she knows are on each page. Child finds specific words that have been recalled, based on child's memory of the storyline, using picture cues, sight words, and letter knowledge.

- Child may finger-point read words in familiar predictable books. Child tracks print by pointing to individual words while reading memorized portions of text.

- Child has a larger set of sight words.

- Child still uses clues seen at the consolidating level, but relies more heavily on print cues than on others (e.g., looks at beginning letter, and perhaps at other letters, in the printed word, and attempts to sound out some words).

Print Understanding and Use

Skill	Rubric Level		
	Beginning	**Consolidating**	**Proficient**
Alphabet Letter Knowledge Child's knowledge of the letter names and shapes, and their understanding about the relationship between letters and the sounds they typically represent	Child's letter knowledge is confined primarily to some letters in the child's own name, and awareness of sounds in words is confined to contexts in which adults isolate them.	Child's knowledge of many uppercase letters, improving awareness of the distinctive shapes of letters, and increasing range of sounds linked to letter names.	Child's knowledge of uppercase letters and some lowercase letters increases along with increasing ability to relate letters to the sounds they represent, including use of analogy between sight words and new words.
	• Child identifies letters by shape, but cannot name most of them (e.g., can do simple alphabet puzzles, can match uppercase letters when presented in small sets). • Child can name most or all of the letters in own name and the first letters in names of friends or relatives. • Child can point to some letters in the alphabet when an adult names them. • When an adult is writing a word and isolates a sound whose name child knows, child can sometimes name the letter that represents the sound.	• Child is skilled at matching letter shapes for all uppercase letters (e.g., can do uppercase alphabet puzzles) and is able to match lowercase letters when in small sets. • Child can name letters in own name, some letters that appear in classmates' names, and additional distinctive or common letters, especially distinctive ones, such as *A, O, S,* and *X,* but often misnames letters that are visually similar (e.g., *D, P; W, M; E, F*). • Child knows a few lowercase letters, usually those in child's own name, or those that are similar in shape to their uppercase matches. • Child links many sounds that the adult isolates to letters by matching the sound to a letter name. • Child may attempt to sound out first letters in words found in environmental print and familiar books.	• Child can name most or all of the uppercase letters in the alphabet. • Child can name some lowercase letters, such as those in the child's own name, and those that are physically similar to the uppercase letter. Child may confuse names of letters that look alike, especially lowercase *p, q,* and *b, d.* • Child has learned some sound-letter associations that are not based on letter-name knowledge (e.g., *sh* for first sound in *ship, ch* for first sound in *chair, w* for first sound in *wand*). • Child often analyzes sounds in words and writes letters that have a relationship to the sounds. Child may use knowledge of sound-letter relationships in known words to determine sound-letter relationships in new words (e.g., Abigail spells first sound in *apple* with *A;* Eliot spells first sound in *egg* with *E*).

How to Complete the Rubrics, Summary Form, and Child Information Sheet

Think of the language and literacy rubrics as a lens through which you will view and record observations about children.

Preparation

- Carefully review the rubrics, preferably as part of an in-service professional development experience. If this is not possible, meet as a classroom team and discuss the meanings of the items and strategies you might use to observe the behaviors that are described.

- Create an assessment/portfolio folder for each child in your class. Include a copy of the rubrics in each child's portfolio. Also, consider how you will decide what materials and/or observational notes get collected and when. Cross-reference your activity plans with the rubrics to ensure that you will have information that will allow you to address each scale on the rubrics.

- On an ongoing basis, collect information that documents a child's current performance in each skill area. File documentation of the child's development such as anecdotal records and work samples in the portfolio. Devise methods to make quick notes about abilities described on the rubrics that are reflected in work samples or observed behaviors. You might find that it is efficient to use the back of the rubrics to make notes about a child. Create a system that allows you to record the date, the observation, initial interpretations or comments, and the initials of the person who made the observation. Identify work samples with the child's name and the date.

- Ensure that your program has procedures for storing rubrics and portfolios in a location where all classroom staff have access to them and can contribute observations or work samples. Arrange for systematic collection of information about children from other staff who may not be in the classroom with children regularly.

- While you will be observing children on an ongoing basis, there may be a need to focus your information gathering on one or more areas as a part of classroom activities. Remember to be objective and unobtrusive as you observe.

- Plan regular and frequent times for staff to discuss children's progress and at these meetings have portfolios and rubrics available so that comments or work samples can be added and reviewed with ease. Refer to rubrics to check on children's progress.

- It is recommended that three times a year, you schedule time for all staff who work with the child regularly to pull together all information about the child and complete the Summary Forms, using the steps that follow.

- Decisions about each child's progress should be based on the documentation in his or her portfolio. It is also recommended that staff, while filling out the Summary Forms, be prepared to record information about the quality of the data assembled for each child.

- As a program, devise a systematic means of sharing information with parents. The complete rubrics are likely to be overwhelming to parents, but do strive to provide parents honest and clear information about their child's progress. Examples from a portfolio are very effective ways to communicate evidence of a child's growth.

Completing the Summary Form

- It is recommended you complete Summary Forms for each child three times a year. You may consider completing the Summary Forms after Units 2, 4, and 6.

- Reproduce the Summary Form and the Child Information Sheet.

- Assemble all accumulated information relevant to rating a child's progress.

- Strive to ensure input from as many people as possible. Evaluations may be completed by an individual teacher or by all classroom staff working together as a team. Group input is preferable and should draw upon the information that has been accumulated in the child's portfolio.

- Review each rubric, ensure that everyone understands what is being evaluated, and consult relevant documentation in the child's portfolio.

- For each rubric, determine which level best characterizes the child's current status: *Beginning, Consolidating,* or *Proficient*. Determining the level will often be based on having observations of behaviors on multiple occasions. The strength of the data (e.g., work samples, informal assessment) also can figure into the decision-making process. Note that each point on the continuum on a rubric describes several behaviors that tend to go together. Individual children will show distinct patterns of development. You should decide which description best depicts a child.

  - **Beginning:** Child is at an early point of mastering the competencies described. Some abilities are present, but they may be fragile, appearing in some contexts and not in others. Often teacher support is required.

  - **Consolidating:** Child is gaining control of competencies described. Abilities are often displayed, but not consistently or only in certain contexts. Teacher support may be needed to display high-level abilities.

  - **Proficient:** Child consistently and independently displays control of the abilities described.

- Note the sources of information used to rate the child on each skill. Categories for describing the kinds of information are as follows:

  - Note = Notes made after observing the behavior

  - W-S = Work samples or portfolio

  - Mem = Memory of the teacher

  - P-R = Parent report

  - I-A = Informal assessment, teacher administered (describe)

- Note the general level of confidence you have in this evaluation, given the available data. For example, a work sample or anecdotal record clearly noting a given behavior is strong data whereas a partial recollection is relatively weak. Teams also should consider how often a behavior has been observed. It is recommended that a team check a child as displaying a given behavior at least on three or four occasions, and notes made about areas worthy of special mention.

- Identify areas of particular weakness and consider whether the identified weakness reveals persistent problems or if it either has only recently been recognized or only recently became apparent. Determine actions to be taken to address areas of concern, including the possibility of conducting more frequent reviews of this aspect of development.

- Identify areas of particular strength. Consider whether the child is being challenged in those areas where strengths are noted. Develop plans for ensuring appropriate levels of challenge.

- Develop an action plan and share it with all staff who work with the child.

- Meet with parents to share observations and discuss plans for supporting the child's continued development.

Completing the Child Information Sheet

- Use child information and the Summary Form to complete the top section of the Child Information Sheet.

- Refer to the Summary Form to complete the bottom section of the Information Sheet. Summarize the child's general development level. Highlight areas of special strengths and weaknesses. Record the action plan or next steps you've determined for the child.

Uses of Summary Information

The primary use of the language and literacy rubrics is to enable teachers to track children's development and tailor instruction to their needs. Another valuable use for the data is as a basis for talking with parents about their child's progress. As teachers discuss the child's performance using the Summary Form, parents will learn about their child and gain greater understanding of the developmental domains that foster early literacy development. Data also can be used to provide summaries of the status of all the children in a teacher's classroom at one point in time, and over time. The overall assessment of all children in a classroom may be passed to program administrators to use for program accountability purposes.

Once Summary Forms have been completed and decisions made about the child's general developmental status in different domains, this information should be incorporated into whatever broader assessment system is in use by the early childhood program.

Child Information Sheet

Child's Name: _____ Date of Birth: _____

Gender: _____ Male _____ Female I.E.P.: _____

Home Language(s): _____

Center/School: _____ Teacher: _____

Date Review Completed: _____ Expected Date of Next Review: _____

Person(s) Completing Review: _____

Summary of Language and Literacy Development *Make reference to rubrics to indicate the child's general developmental level. Note areas of special strength and weakness.*

Action Steps and Recommendations:

SUMMARY FORM

Child's Name:

Domain/Area of Development	Rubric Level B: Beginning C: Consolidating P: Proficient	Sources of Information	Comments
Oral Language			
Vocabulary			
Conversation			
Using Language to Resolve Conflicts			
Using Language to Tell Personal Narratives and Engage in Pretend Play			
Using Language to Learn Information and How to Do Things			
Learning Information			

SUMMARY FORM

Child's Name:

Assessment   1   2   3

Domain/Area of Development	Rubric Level B: Beginning C: Consolidating P: Proficient	Sources of Information	Comments
Phonological Awareness			
Syllable Awareness			
Beginning Sounds			
Rhyme Awareness			
Phonemic Awareness			

SUMMARY FORM

Child's Name:

Assessment 1 2 3

Domain/Area of Development	Rubric Level B: Beginning C: Consolidating P: Proficient	Sources of Information	Comments
Book Interest and Understanding			
Interest in Books			
Understanding of and Responses to Books			
Print Understanding and Use			
Meaning and Uses of Print			
Early Writing			
Early Reading			
Alphabet Letter Knowledge			